PRAI[illegible]

MW01679300

In your hands you hold the key strategies and insights for making it on your own. Never easy, always rewarding when you work through the challenges you will face. Sue shares what you need to know and what you need to do to become a Small Business Solo Success story of your own!

Mark LeBlanc
Author, Never Be the Same and Growing Your Business!

This book is hugely beneficial for entrepreneurs who need a measuring guide to succeed. Both practical and inspiring, Sue shares a wealth of wisdom amplified by her own personal experiences.

Les and Fran Hewitt, Author, The Power of Focus

Almost anybody interested in making it on their own as a Solopreneuer will find golden nuggets here. You will want to refer to this highly readable book again and again.

Henry DeVries
Co-Author, How to Close a Deal Like Warren Buffett

This book will significantly shorten your learning curve as you progress to success.

Penny Reed
Author, Growing Your Dental Business

As the CHO of the #1 RE/MAX office in the world, I am very happy to see a book of this calibre for real estate agents and Solopreneurs alike! You can't learn these kinds of strategies at school; it takes years of experience and the willingness to share. Sue has coached many agents and team leaders in our office and presented her insights at our meetings, and I am confident in the value this book offers.

Nick JM Profeta
Manager/Associate, CHO (Chief Happiness Officer)
RE/MAX Real Estate (Central)

The Little Red Stick is a must-read for any solo business owner, particularly those in the competitive world of real estate who are looking to master the skills to succeed on a daily basis. In this fun, advice-filled book, Sue Styles helps business owners discover how to leverage their talents and assets in order to be more effective. I recommend this book to anyone looking to grow their business with less stress, and more finesse, and to have so many of the tools they need to grow their business all in one place.

Alan Samuel Cohen
Author, The Connection Challenge™:
How to Create Power and Possibility in the Age of Distraction

The Little RED Stick

WHAT GETS MEASURED, GETS DONE!

SIMPLE STRATEGIES
FOR MASTERING SOLO SUCCESS

The Little RED Stick

WHAT GETS MEASURED, GETS DONE!

ISBN: 978-0-9868225-2-0

For more information, please write to the publisher at:
Sue@MaximizedResults.com

PRINTED IN CANADA

The author designed the information to represent her opinions about the subjects disclosed. The reader must weigh carefully all aspects of any personal decisions before making any changes in his or her business. The author obtained the information contained through research and experience.

The author speaks from her perspective and experience and believes her advice is sound. The author disclaims any liability, loss or risk incurred by individuals who act on the information enclosed.

I dedicate this book to my family,
who were my cheerleaders and open ears.
If someone had discouraged me, I think I would have given up! But all of your faith in me gave me faith in myself. For that I am forever grateful and blessed!

To Jamie, Tammy, Steve, and Mom (Barbara), and to my children, Amy, Kaila, Vince, and Sara.

Also to my extended family fans,
Aunty Gayle, Uncle Jim and Aunty Lynn.

Either accept conditions as they exist,
or accept responsibility for changing them.

Denis Waitley

TABLE OF CONTENTS

The Little RED Stick

This is more than a book.
It's a system, a process that will teach you how to get any results you want in business so that you are not only working efficiently, but also working effectively toward maximized results!

The Little RED Stick

One spring my husband took me on an amazing trip to meet his brother and his family in Lafayette, Louisiana. Along with their heartfelt Southern hospitality was their willingness to tell us all about their State and the attractions it has to offer.

We took a boat ride on a dark, muddy bayou river and saw alligators basking in the weeds. We stuffed ourselves with crawfish (when I say "we," I actually mean my husband since I just couldn't get my head around sucking the juices out of the little crustaceans!). But my favourite outing was our visit to Avery Island.

Avery Island is the one place in the whole world where Tabasco© is made, and if you have never had the pleasure of visiting, I would highly encourage it! The island hosts a breathtaking sanctuary for birds and alligators as well as lush vegetation and old-world trees. It is here that they create and bottle their hot sauce in a production plant, and one can visit an impressive store with everything branded and shouting the hot sauce's promise.

As my husband and I toured the Tabasco plant and facility, a young woman explained to us how Tabasco is made. The Tabasco pepper is much like the green pepper in that as it ripens, it changes colour. At the perfect shade of red, the peppers are picked to be made into the hot sauce. She noted that when new pickers join the team, they aren't familiar with the exact shade of red the pepper needs to be to result in the perfect sauce. If they pick peppers that are too light in colour, the sauce could end up bitter; if they pick them too late, they will be overripe. So the owners, the McIhenneys, came up with the idea of a little red stick, which they call "Le Petite Baton Rouge," painted the exact shade of red that the ripe pepper needs to be.

When the new pickers go out into the fields, they tuck the stick into their work belt and use it to easily measure the colour of the pepper until they are practised and precise in their picking. Learning with this tool keeps the standard of the product high and allows the company to continue to grow. The McIhenneys have been in the business of providing excellence for over 100 years! The Tabasco company is clear on what they want, they are pro-active, and they make sure their standards are achieved.

Think about your own business.

What measures do you have in place to ensure that everything is done right? When you hire new people, do you have standards that they can measure their performance against?

Think about each stage of your business from the time you meet a new customer until he or she is sending you referrals. If you create your own "Little Red Stick," you can ensure that the standards you want your company to measure up to are met!

As the saying goes, "What gets measured, gets done."

How Can I Help You?

My mission is to help Solopreneurs like you to become as successful as you want to be in your business. I want to be a catalyst in raising the success rate of agents in the real estate industry from a mere 13 percent to over 25 percent over the next decade. And if the typical Solopreneur has a 10 percent chance of finding success, I want to double the odds and show you the way. If you know a business, a brokerage, or a company that needs me, please help us connect.

That is my business goal.

I have noticed that as I find the freedom to do more of what I enjoy, my heart always goes back to the single mom I used to be. I remember the help I wished I'd had during some hard years, and I now take every opportunity to help single parents. I try to be the change I want to see in the world. I have found that the more successful I have become, the more I realize that I really do have more than enough, and the more I find joy in reaching out to help someone else.

I want to help YOU, so that you can turn around and help others. I want you to reach a level where you are celebrating your successes, have more than enough money, and can help those who are on your own heart.

SECTION I

WHY STRIVE FOR SOLO SUCCESS?

CHAPTER 1

Think Like a Solopreneur; Act Like a Boss

My mini-van smelled of stale beer and sticky pop as I drove to the recycling depot with bags of empty cans to make some money. The depot was in the middle of the city on a busy street. As I pulled in and parked, I saw myself in the homeless who were hanging around the front. It hit me like a sloppy slap in the face—ENOUGH! I couldn't live like this anymore!

I was at the recycling depot because it was my son's twelfth birthday, and I had no money for a party. He was number three out of my four children, and his birthday unfortunately came up right in the middle of my losing streak.

I felt like a failure as a parent with no hope for a trip to Chucky Cheese's with a group of his young friends. The last birthday party I threw (before my divorce and bankruptcy) I hired a limo to surprise my youngest daughter and all her friends for a trip around the city—with all the bells and whistles. But this birthday party had to be different.

I had asked my son what kind of food he would like for his birthday, appealing to the stomach of a tween, and he told me Chinese Food.

Oh great, I thought, the one food I can't really cook myself. Why couldn't he have said Italian! Pasta I could cook for pennies!

I was determined that if I couldn't offer him a party or a present, then at least he could have the food he asked for. I went to my neighbours' and humbled myself enough to ask whether they had any empties. That resulted in two bags of stinky cans which gave me just enough money for an order of ginger beef and one order of noodles. At home, I cooked up a big pot of rice.

That was as good as it got that year.

Have you ever been at a place in your life where you just throw up your hands and shout "ENOUGH!"?

Whether you've been there for a while or have just hit a wall recently, I've been there, my friend, and I believe I can offer you what I needed myself at the time—HOPE.

No matter whether things are all good or all bad, they never stay the same. Remember that the tide WILL turn, and in the meantime, perhaps I can help you kick the tide and get the results that you need right now.

It is time to Think Like a Solopreneur; Act Like a Boss

Who am I?

I have been enjoying a Solopreneur career for many years. I started in the real estate industry, working as support for the very best agents in our city. I learned the sharpest systems and developed tactical processes so that our multi-million-dollar offices could keep up with the volume of business. When I went out on my own, coaching and consulting for real estate agents, I started helping other Solopreneurs take their businesses up a level by changing their habits and setting up plans that allowed them to take action.

I was asked by my local real estate board to help with writing a two-day course for support staff. I also wrote my own course, "So You're a REALTOR®, Now What?", for new agents, which I have offered regularly. I wrote a book, *Be Extraordinary—Right Where You Are!*, for Administrative Assistants, which has been sold at the National Association for REALTORS® conference multiple times. I also speak to local brokerages, to teams, at educational events, and still enjoy coaching one-on-one.

The road I started on was steep and difficult. I started from LESS than nothing because after my divorce, I went bankrupt. I can honestly say I quadrupled my income within two years! Of course, being bankrupt at the beginning, four times almost nothing wasn't that hard!

Over the years of teaching, I realized that one of the best ways to help many more budding Solopreneurs—who have ideas for a business and a yearning to control their own success—would be to write a book about the main keys I preach. These keys teach how to set up systems, how to use scalable processes, how to invite in customers, and how to achieve the ultimate mastery of becoming a true "Boss," one who takes purposeful time working ON his or her business rather than just IN it.

Let's begin this ride by having you spend five minutes giving yourself an overview of your business. I'm BIG on getting RESULTS, but if you don't know where the holes are, it's kind of hard to plug and fix them, right? So here are some areas in which to rate your business. If there are others I haven't included, just write them in. Use this book to its fullest capacity!

Rate Yourself on a scale of 1 to 10 with 10 being working with excellence and exactness.

Your Brand and Image to the world—How great is your website, social media, and product that you sell?

1 2 3 4 5 6 7 8 9 10

Lead Conversion—How is your lead generation? Is your marketing causing the calls to come in? When someone calls, are you able to connect with them immediately and make an appointment?

1 2 3 4 5 6 7 8 9 10

Business Processes—How is your big picture process from beginning to end? Is there common sense flow and are you being pro-active (as opposed to reactive)?

1 2 3 4 5 6 7 8 9 10

Checklists and Systems—Do you have systems in place for each stage of the process? Are they detailed enough that you can delegate to an assistant when the time comes?

1 2 3 4 5 6 7 8 9 10

Client Care—From a new lead to active client, and then afterwards for years to come until you are receiving referrals, are you doing everything you can?

1 2 3 4 5 6 7 8 9 10

Marketing and Advertising—Do you have an annual plan that gives results and allows you to project manage and implement with precision?

1 2 3 4 5 6 7 8 9 10

Using the results from this exercise, you can begin to focus on the lower numbers so you can improve your business significantly. Have you ever done an exercise like this before? If YOU just took a moment in doing this test to work ON your business rather than just IN it, then good for you!

For those of you who routinely evaluate yourself, this probably didn't take long and may have confirmed some things you might have already known.

I find that if you have questions and needs to begin with, you are more likely to get better results when reading something, whether it's this book, a business manual, the newspaper, or a spiritual book.

The answers are all around us if we just look for them!

Throughout this book, I am going to share many of my experiences and stories. If you have questions, comments, or your own stories, please get involved online and share them through my online group at www.suestyles.com. Your question or comment may help someone—and I love the collaboration!

Everyday Mindful Millionaires

I have had the good pleasure to break bread with some fine leaders. As a journalist at heart, I always enjoy hearing the inside scoop on how success is attained. I had all this value at my fingertips, but if I just kept all the wealthy seas of knowledge to myself, what good would it be? Sure, I can use the information in my work with clients, but that is only one person at a time. So, throughout this book are seven of my best interviews with some hard-working, everyday mindful millionaires who share their truth and wisdom (some over coffee, some as I listened to the entrepreneurs share on the platform).

Nick JM Profeta,
CHO (Chief Happiness Officer)
RE/MAX Real Estate (Central)

QUESTION: Nick, what is the best way to become a successful REALTOR®? Do you need to be an A-type personality?

You don't have to be any one type of personality. The key is to be the absolute very best you. Learn to be authentic, be earnest; convince yourself that you ARE the best service provider and others will believe it too.

If you are not naturally aggressive, don't try to force the sales. You will attract the same type of person as yourself. The world is not made up of just one kind of person! Do your best to bring enjoyment to what you are doing and focus on your clients; ask yourself what the consumer needs and wants—then give it to them.

Once you hit 24 to 30 deals, seriously consider starting to hire out administrative tasks. Stop spending too much time doing the things you don't enjoy and spend more time working with your clients. The value of hiring an assistant will far outweigh the cost to the business—in fact, it should result in your being free to bring in more business as your support staff takes over more and more duties.

CHAPTER 2

Solo Success Takes Brains, Heart, and Courage

Have you ever watched the movie, The Wizard of Oz? I know the moral of the story is "There's no place like home." But I can also see fabulous principles for business success in this much-loved movie.

Allow me to share this classic from another angle!

When Dorothy sets out to attain her goal of reaching the Emerald City, she encounters three characters along the way. I think these characters display the perfect characteristics we need in our businesses.

Dorothy first happens upon the Scarecrow. What does he represent? Brains. He needs to find a brain. In any business, there is an undeniable need for intelligence, common sense, book learning, and street smarts. The first thing you want to assess in your own business is this:

1. What do I need to learn right now? What information and knowledge would help me increase my value?

Take 60 seconds and come up with at least one thing that would improve your ability to move forward.

____

____

____

Dorothy then comes across the Tin Man. He is missing his heart; he's stuck and can't move.

2. What about you? Are you halted in your tracks or losing steam? Have you lost your passion, or are you in touch with the heart of your business, WHY you are doing this in the first place?

I have hosted many workshops on reconnecting with your "Big Why," because often as soon as the busyness of the work takes over, we lose our closeness to the core of what drives our success. Being in touch with your "Why" is so important that icons, such as Dr. John DeMartini, have built a career around it. Robin Sharma preaches about it and Simen Sinek became famous for his "Ted Talk" about it. Feeling the passion beneath the vision is a necessary step in building lasting growth and success.

Setting material needs aside, what was it that compelled you to choose this particular business?

If you aren't clear on WHY you are spending 24/7 on your business, you will not be able to endure.

This week might be the perfect time to remind yourself and your team of the story behind your personal "need to succeed."

Why do you want this?

As Dorothy and her new friends make their way closer to the Emerald City, they are surprised by a big lion and even more surprised that he lacks courage!

3. I want you to take a moment to think about where you need to take a risk to advance your business. What is it that scares you?

One exercise I enjoy doing with groups is the following:

> Think of someone you know who is brave enough to do anything he or she wants.
>
> ____
>
> ____
>
> If you were this person, what would you have the courage to do?
>
> ____
>
> ____
>
> Ask yourself whether there is a risk you need to take in order to get to the next level and, if so, what is it?
>
> ____
>
> ____
>
> You now have three tangible answers that will direct you in creating a better business! Excellent work!

You Have To Try UNTIL

When I finally got a job in the entrepreneurial world of real estate, I didn't know much about that kind of work or life. I had been a prenatal teacher while having my own four children, and then hosted a local TV cable tourism show. So, my own preconceptions of the industry were very

Hollywood-based, filled with putting exciting deals together, million-dollar homes, fancy cars, and nice clothes. My entry-level job with the first REALTOR® confirmed my expectations in some respects. It entailed a fast-paced work style and an even faster paced lifestyle for my boss.

I was lucky to start out with someone at the top and could see, over the years, the vast chasm between those who made it and those who were struggling to stay afloat.

After working with several top sales agents and multi-million-dollar teams for about five years, I took the licensing course myself and started teaching what I had learned about the actual running of the business.

I confirmed what I had seen first-hand—getting your license does not set you up to run a successful business! New sales agents needed to be shown how to do a listing presentation, set up their systems and begin a useful database. But it wasn't just newbies who needed my help. I found that even when I began to consult with a high-level team, there were always things that could be tightened up, new ideas that would help keep the clients connected, or marketing that could be done better.

As I met more and more agents in the real estate industry and then began teaching courses at the local Board, I couldn't help seeing that they needed help in their businesses, whether they were new or had been at it for thirty years! My passion to help the Solopreneur was born and has been growing ever since!

I began to do some research into the real estate industry as my own consulting business grew. The numbers from the Canadian Real Estate Council showed some shockingly bad news. I learned that over a span of five years (from 2010 to 2015), about 60 percent of real estate agents were

GROSSING between $0 and $60,000 on between 0 and 12 deals per year. About 30 percent were bringing in between 12 and 25 deals a year, and only the top 10 percent were closing more than 26 deals a year. Yet, I had been working with those who were regularly closing 100 to 300 deals each year and making it look easy. But the statistics showed a different overall story.

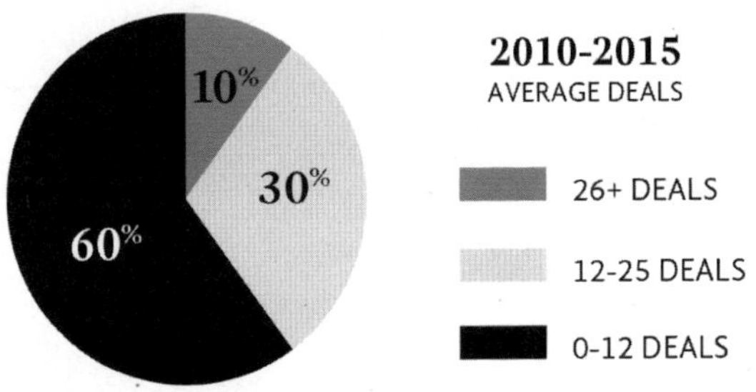

The National Association of REALTORS® (NAR) posted a study that showed a dismal 87 percent failure rate in the industry with only 13 percent of agents still in business after 5 years.

These statistics are similar in other entrepreneurial and solopreneurial businesses, whether the individual is a hairdresser, bookkeeper, graphic designer, journalist, mortgage broker, or sales agent in a different industry. And the message I got was loud and clear: Stay Away from Solopreneurship! It's too hard. Chances are slim. There's no pay for sick days, your children will take second place to your clients, and you'll constantly be interrupted by phone calls. And, if commissions are only paid after a deal has closed, you could be starving for months waiting for some income.

Being a Solopreneur is different from being an employee—no one tells you what to do or what quota to meet.

You have no help, and it's up to you to become the expert in everything!

- Website
- Social media
- Marketing
- Selling
- Administration
- Negotiations

Not to mention . . .

- It's hard to stay accountable for what needs to be done.
- Your phone won't ring automatically—and when it does, you may not be well enough organized to handle each deal with ease.
- You think you will just figure it out as you go, but when it's not going, you can't figure it out—and if it takes off, you don't have time to prepare!
- You don't know where to find clients.
- You may not have three years of income saved up to support yourself as you struggle to pull together enough deals to stand on your own.
- You may have a lot of ideas, but no money to implement them because you haven't closed enough deals to show a profit.
- You also may have too many ideas to know what to do first, and suffer paralysis by analysis.

What else is hard for you? Write it down. Let's put all the cards on the table.

____

____

____

I can relate. I have seen the same struggle occur in careers and in personal lives. For example, when I got divorced, I moved and brought my four children (ages 5 to 13) to the big city where I had landed a new job in sales. Of course, they hated to move, and my first job turned out to be less than desirable.

I quit within the year, and my next job was even worse with a playa manager who cheated on his wife and traded porn with his male counterparts. The owner of this strategic equity firm had a turnover of 120 percent while I worked there (he was not well-liked). I was completely out of my zone, didn't know there was a game to be played, and finally quit a company that seemed to be going down some strange rabbit hole that I didn't want to be any part of.

Then I couldn't find a job.
I couldn't pay my bills.
I ended up in bankruptcy.

At this point I wanted to give up, throw in the towel, go home to mommy. I was finished and had no more ideas of how to make life work. My desire to be a stay-at-home mom had ended; there was no husband to pay the bills or support the family. My ex was depressed, unemployed, and unattainable, and soon my employment insurance would run out.

This was a new low for me.

Of course, I sent out resumés. Certainly, my acquaintances knew I needed work and would let me know if they heard of anything. But nothing was happening. I tried—and nothing.

Except, this wasn't just for me; I had four children who needed me to come through for *them*.

At my lowest point, depressed and hopeless, I did what a lot of people who are down do—I went to Starbucks. I moped around Indigo/Chapters for about an hour and was just about to leave when a book caught my eye. I was drawn by its black cover. I picked it up and flipped to a random page. I was still angry and frustrated, and I dared the book to tell me something! My eyes caught these words on the page: THINGS DON'T ALWAYS WORK OUT. SOMETIMES YOU HAVE TO MAKE THEM WORK OUT.

When I read that, I had such an aha moment! I mulled it over. Sometimes things don't work out. That is what Dr Henry Cloud was telling me in his book.

I learned a great lesson through this: it wasn't up to me to just try once, or send out resumés for any jobs I could find. It was up to me to try UNTIL.

I had to keep looking and keep talking to people and keep searching online UNTIL I got an interview and UNTIL I actually got offered a job.

My advice to you, as an entrepreneur, is this: keep trying UNTIL it works.

You have to try UNTIL.

Because it probably won't work at first. It might not even work the second try. In fact, it could be months before you get into the swing of your business. You must change your mindset and become someone who will try UNTIL.

Amy's Story

Amy became a REALTOR® a few years ago. Between the licensing program, starting with a brokerage, and then buying signs, paying dues, etc., she had invested around $10,000.00. She burst out of the gate with high hopes that she could recover her investment within the year.

But putting her feet on the pavement and taking action to make sales didn't come easily. Where could she start?

She told everyone she was an agent. Her close friends and family congratulated her, but they didn't hire her. She was too new. Naturally, when buyers and sellers are trading hundreds of thousands of dollars in real estate, they may not feel confident having a newbie negotiating their investment!

Amy considered what she should do about that roadblock. So, in her second year (with only two deals behind her), she decided to try to find a successful team that could back her up with their experience and pass along some leads. Finally, she found some lovely people and joined their group. She liked the occasional meetings and camaraderie, she got a couple of leads, she closed a deal, and then the momentum halted. Summer season came and the business seemed to dry up for the agents, and they weren't passing any more leads along.

Discouraged, but not ready to give up, she left that team and joined one of the top teams in her city. The team was in the top 10 and had systems in place and a business model that fed tons of leads to their agents every day! She knew a lack of leads had been the obstacle to her success, so she started calling the leads as soon as they came in online. It was all about lead capture and volume.

Although she was getting more leads, many of them were from immigrants. These leads brought with them language and financial barriers; often potential clients were simply "kicking tires," unable to qualify for mortgages. Amy was so busy chasing the wind that she wasn't doing her own marketing or taking the time to make her own connections.

Her money started running out. She needed to make some personal choices that would help her on her tiny budget (like moving in with her brother and sister), just so she could keep going.

The third year, Amy was desperate for sales and determined to make her real estate business work! After only closing a couple more deals, she decided she should try another team, more aligned with her own style of working with clients. She was lucky enough to get in with the number one team in a local RE/MAX Brokerage firm and pulled herself up by her bootstraps once again.

But then her car bit the dust, and she couldn't afford to get it fixed.

Now, anyone watching Amy's journey would have told her, "Hey, you've given it a good try. But don't you think it's time to go and get a regular job so that you can pay your bills, get a car, and live a life? This isn't working, and it doesn't look like it's going to get any better. Not everyone is meant to be an entrepreneur. It's hard. You tried; be proud of that. But it's time to throw in the towel, don't you think?"

No one would have faulted Amy if she had ended up changing direction. After all, 87 percent of agents do just that.

But that was not Amy's dream. Something happened when Amy came to the end of her rope—she tied a knot and held on.

In the new team, she decided that she was going to act as if she were busy and successful. That meant changing her habits and for one thing, going in to the office every day and "working." That was a challenge since her car had quit, but she didn't let that stop her. She got out her bike, put on her helmet each morning, and pedalled the 45 minutes to work.

She joined in with whatever was going on, she made calls, she helped with deals, she processed files, she got her hands into the business. When an agent presented an offer, she joined in; when there was a listing presentation she tagged along. She took it all in by osmosis and started generating her own wheel of motion by following the steps and schedules of the busy agents on her team.

She got a client. Then another. After her first year with the RE/MAX team, she had closed 12 deals. She bought a car that looked nice enough to present a good image, but cost little enough that she could afford the payments. After four years as a licensed REALTOR®, she had finally acquired the habits of a business work style and was making money at what she loved doing.

And isn't that the beauty of being a Solopreneur—doing what you love? Even though I listed many reasons for NOT becoming an entrepreneur, those of you still reading have that fire in your belly that makes you want to be successful doing what you want to do! Good for you! Stay with me and I will help you navigate the yellow brick road to your own Emerald City.

Remind yourself what it is that you want to accomplish in your business. As I often say at conferences, I believe that most of us are just one daily habit away from reaching our goals. We can become anything we want to be! I could become a doctor, midwife, meteorologist, writer, mechanic, etc. All it takes is doing the things each and every day that will result in getting you there.

When you feel like you've got nothing to lose,
then nothing can stand in your way.

How Can You Succeed as A Solopreneur?

Let me ask you this: do your daily habits match your yearly goals? This is the bottom line and where "the rubber meets the road." This is where success is lost or found.

Listen, I believe you can make it and stay in the top 13 percent with the right business habits. But, if you will allow me to help you turn your business into your best success, I believe you can absolutely make it to the top 3 percent and truly enjoy the lifestyle that probably drew you into the business in the first place!

If you take the time to put your full attention on each chapter of this book, you will get an immediate Return on Your Investment (ROI).

- You will learn practical applications you can take to your office and begin implementing immediately.
- You will create a plan to maximize your income potential.
- You will discover steps you might have missed.
- You will cut the learning curve time in half and fast-track to closing deals!
- You will fill in any gaps that have been missing from your systems and processes.
- You will gain mastery as a Solopreneur!

I want to help you to burn bright—not burn out!

Everyday Mindful Millionaires

Mark Stephen, Business Entrepreneur,
Martinizing by Stephen (*Dry Cleaners*)

Advice for Entrepreneurs!

- Deliver on your promises.
- Ask clients what THEY want; don't assume and don't be afraid to ask. Then meet and exceed expectations.
- Hire exceptional people who will give exceptional service.
- Take opportunities to turn issues into Gold Star Experiences for clients.

It's Not All in Your Head

Have you seen the movie, The Secret? Great movie. It gave me a lot of direction during those years of single parenting and going through bankruptcy—but it left me just one step short of success. It couldn't tell me the action steps to take to get to where I wanted to go. My mind was positive, my vibes were loving, I imagined a great life—but I didn't know how to put it into action.

Let me illustrate: One spring, I was determined to lose some weight and become healthy before summer arrived. After thinking about it for weeks, I started going on a run every day—well, every other day—well, sometimes I just ran for the first minute and then walked the rest of the way . . .

After two weeks, I was disappointed that I couldn't see any results. I had been consciously thinking about losing weight for a month! I had bought some healthy food and had eaten it (along with some other things—but I ignored the cheese buns and wine). I honestly felt that I had been really concentrating on getting healthy and was frustrated that it wasn't happening!

That was when I had an aha moment!

I see entrepreneurs doing this in their businesses all the time! So much thought and intention goes into a process, and it's so mentally strenuous that they feel as if they actually did the work!

When I was trying to lose weight, I was fooling myself into thinking that just envisioning the exercise and healthy eating (like a run and the odd chicken salad) would do the trick! But I was only playing a trick on myself—and so are you when you buy into the easy way.

It will never be enough to just imagine all the healthy meals you could replace your fast food with; you must actually do it. It will never be enough to schedule into your calendar each day a morning run but only do half of it; you have to do enough work to make a difference!

And that was when I recognized that in our businesses we need to realize this too.

I meet with many clients who talk as if they have lots on the go, deals left and right, and they have ideas they are taking to the bank. The trouble is, when I see what is actually happening in their business, it might be less than half of what they THINK they are doing.

Can you identify with that in your own life or business?

Positive intention is a great tool, but it is just a part of the whole story. Yes, you should envision a successful business; yes, you should intend towards your goals, have them written on your vision board, etc. But it's your daily habits that you need to change into daily action that will fulfill your grand intentions.

Your daily habits determine your yearly results.

Let's take an example of a woman I was working with not too long ago. She was new to the real estate business but had a long corporate career. So, she did know some core principles of business.

The first thing I noticed was that her online profile suffered—from hardly being there! We reviewed three social media platforms, and I advised her to have a professional photo taken, write a biography, and get some connections.

We spent three weeks working on her biography, and then she asked her son to take a new photo of her. By week four, she had created one online profile and gotten her hair cut and styled. I know that she felt as if she had done a lot of work, and it certainly was ten times better than what she had had, but it wasn't nearly finished!

Her two or three actions towards the change made her feel as if she had accomplished her to-do list. This was more than she had ever done online so she was proud of herself. I was proud of her too, but also determined to keep her accountable until EVERYTHING was done to the best of her ability.

I think we sometimes sell ourselves short on what we are capable of!

Don't stop when you have only nicked the surface of accomplishment. There is a whole mountain to be climbed!

Perhaps your business is suffering simply because you don't actually KNOW how to put better systems in place. Perhaps with just a tweak to your client care, you could see ten times the return. Now that I know what I've learned from the business of real estate and the hard knocks of real life (I consider myself my own kind of "Road Scholar"), I am here to share it with you. I believe that there will be something you will read here that will directly benefit YOUR business.

I am on a mission to see an increase in the success of entrepreneurs and Solopreneurs! Let's increase your success!

It starts here; it starts now.

It is never too late to be what you might have been.

George Eliot

The most important piece of advice that I can offer is to encourage ACTION. Anyone can have a good idea, but not everyone can implement it. That is where entrepreneurs find success, where they can make things happen. They plan, they consider, and then they execute.

Many times in one-on-one sessions with my clients, we clarify what actual actions are needed—once I show them what to do and how to do it, they can do it on their own.

I have discovered that the most successful real estate agents have key principles in common, and this would apply to any Solopreneurs.

What are the main areas of action that lead to this million-dollar success, you ask? I have broken it into five key practices, habits if you will, that you can measure your own business against. Even though I have worked primarily in the real estate industry, these business truths are relevant cross-industry and would be helpful to any small business owner!

In all extreme achievers there are two things in common, it's about action and all about execution, nothing happens till you move.

Robin Sharma

SECTION II

FIVE DAILY HABITS THAT DRIVE PROFIT

We all want a perfect game, the best score. We want people to think we have the perfect relationship—"Oh, aren't they the perfect couple." We want people to think that we have the perfect children—"Oh, they never give us trouble, they have hearts of gold." We want perfect teeth, the perfect outfit; we want everybody to think we're "the bomb"!

But I have discovered something for myself that perhaps some of you can relate to—imperfection. I believe there is a gift in IMPERFECTION. It's when we acknowledge our need for help, when we can ask for help, when we can admit that everything isn't perfect that we can connect better and grow.

In my business, when REALTORS® and entrepreneurs tell me what they suck at, what's NOT going well, and where they are falling short, THAT'S the moment I can truly help them.

We all want to appear perfect, that we have it all together. But ironically, that is when people feel the least connected to us—and when we strive for that, we just can't go as far in life, being a lone ranger and trying to maintain a perfect image. We can go much further when we get help from others. I believe we are better together!

The history of the golf ball gives us a perfect example of how valuable imperfection is!

Did you know that the original golf balls had a smooth, round surface. Players discovered, however, that balls with nicks and indentations from normal use performed better. So, in 1905, golf balls were produced with dimples. They were made with imperfections so that they could go further.

Let me ask you this: Is it when everything in your life is perfect and easy that you are able to build the strength to go far and reach your goals? No, just the opposite! It is when you have to adjust your sails to find the wind, send your roots deeper during the drought, and press through the storm that you develop the strength and fortitude and find the support to go further. It's when you are struggling and need to become resourceful that you learn how far you can go—what you are capable of! Count the struggle as a blessing.

The struggle gives us the opportunity to become coaches to one another—whether we need to develop a better golf game, build a better business, or become a better parent, partner, or a better person. You have been "dimpled" so you can take your business and your life where you want it to go! Your past has built the trajectory to get you where your focus is. Please don't become discouraged or give up hope—the world needs you!

So, whatever stage you are at right now, be encouraged! I have worked with the best of the best and a couple of the worst, and I can assure you that no matter where you are today, you can move forward tomorrow with a new outlook, some new skills, and new success.

You can do a better business!

Everyday Mindful Millionaires

Marilyn Jones, REALTOR® Calgary, Alberta

Marilyn Jones is the longest working agent I personally know (over 40 years)! She has been president of her Board, an active volunteer, and is still selling real estate today.

She started out as a graduate of secretary school and then worked at a real estate brokerage. In the 1970s she got her license "just in case" anyone needed her help—but then jumped in and learned the business.

Question: What can new agents do to get business?

It took me a long time to get up the courage to send out my first piece of marketing material; I understand how hard it is! I think that door-knocking is back in style. There are lots of good ideas, but like a quote I saw once, "A good idea only works if you do." When I decided to become an active agent, I picked a neighbourhood to farm and sent out my letters. Then came the day I went out knocking on doors to say hello.

I had to get up all my nerve, but I knocked on the first door. The lady opened the door and cheerfully said hello! She happened to know of me because her brother and I had gone to school together, and so she invited me in for tea! I was so relieved with that kind reception that I kept on going.

Marilyn says, "Get going and do it yourself. Get a good piece of marketing material, a single sheet you can hand out. Get organized FIRST and make sure to have your systems in place before you get too busy."

She recounted an experience, early in her career, when she was at the office one day and a few agents were chatting to each other. Her arms were full of books and paperwork and the phone at the reception desk started ringing. The receptionist wasn't there, but no one moved to answer it. The agents may have felt it was beneath them to step in and answer a phone—but not Marilyn! She dropped her books and went over to pick it up—"YOU have to be willing to do everything yourself; it's YOUR job, you must be willing."

If you keep saying "I'm so tired," you will be. If you tell yourself the market is great, it will be. You are your own best cheerleader—or worst enemy!

CHAPTER 3

DAILY HABIT #1: Take Care of Clients Before They Are Clients

It isn't just when someone reaches out to ask questions about your product or service that you need to impress them. You need to impress them before they even think about reaching out to you!

What do you think your reputation is in your industry and in your city?

One afternoon, after teaching a session, I stopped in at the membership department of our local real estate board and chatted with a long-time employee. She asked what office I was working in, and I gave her the REALTOR®'s name. Her immediate response was positive, and she was impressed. She remarked that she had known many agents over the years and usually the wealthy ones, the well-to-do's, the good-looking ones with the fancy clothes and nice cars were arrogant schmucks! They had big egos and were hard to get along with. However, she pointed out how personable and authentically nice the agent I was working with was and how everyone liked her and spoke well of her.

Wow! I was impressed with that reaction!

What do people say behind YOUR back? A reputation can't be fabricated; it is created by what you do behind closed doors—good or bad. Past clients, past employees and industry members are often quick to share their opinions about you and your business.

So, you need to decide what you want others to say about you and then go out and act the part! If you want to be thought of as a leader in your industry, make time to reach back and help others climbing the ladder. If you want potential clients to feel that you will be on their side and go to bat for them, then start doing that right now by negotiating your hardest for your current clients. If it's important that your reputation is one of honesty and integrity, then remember to take actions that are honest and principled when things go wrong or mistakes are made.

It's also worth noting that what goes on behind the scenes is a huge part of what will make or break your reputation. Whether it's your behaviour or your service, studies show that people are eight times more likely to share and talk about negative experiences than they are about positive ones. So, make those positive ones count and keep the negative ones out!

Ideas To Assist You In Building Your Reputation

An obvious area for projecting image and reputation is social media. There are many platforms where you can establish your image with the brand and persona you are hoping to grow into. Here are some things that can help:

- Visual. It is vitally important what your profile picture looks like. I see too many profile and website photos that are from 1989, or that are "selfies" taken in a campground, or are even blurry. I know you have seen them too! But, please, hire a professional photographer and do yourself a favour with an up-to-date, proper photo. It's definitely a necessity and worth the money and attention.

- Brand. Affiliate yourself with products or people that help your brand. I sat down with the owner of a cold-pressed juicing company which skyrocketed to profitable popularity within a short three years. One of the things that the CRU Juice owner told me was how she was able to align the product with other successful brands, such as Holt Renfrew, that were synergistic. The cross-marketing helped others to define her brand quickly.

- Find your words. Stay away from the same ones used over and over again in your industry. Clichés like trustworthy, honest, integrity, "never too busy for your referrals" have been so overused they don't carry any weight anymore. Who are you and what is your service? Put three clear words to it so you and everyone else will know who you are! A team I worked with wanted to make it their goal to become number one in their small town. We went through some branding exercises and came up with the words "reliable, responsive & respectful." They then made it into a promise: "We represent your interests by being reliable, responsive, respectful and ultimately bringing you the results you want!" It is almost their vision statement, and everything they do or post online comes back to this promise and these words.

Everyday Mindful Millionaires

Megan Szanik, Espy

(*Local Fashion Designer's Clothing Store*)

Advice for Entrepreneurs!

- Underpromise and overdeliver.
- Align yourself with exceptional service providers as well as hiring great staff.
- When dealing with upset clients, don't underestimate the power of listening and then bringing in humour!
- Create detailed databases so that clients are known. "Use technology to get personal."

Once you have established your image, it is time to prepare for converting leads when they call. One of the worst regrets I hear from business owners is that they lost a lead. Money in the bank was lost because they weren't ready for the call, were too distracted, or lost the caller's number. Basically, they didn't have a procedure in place to care for potential customers.

As a speaker, I have learned some tricks that help me memorize my speeches so I don't need pages of notes while I'm on stage. One of the tricks is called "mnemonics." You can use this trick when receiving a call out of the blue and aren't prepared with a "Lead Sheet" of your usual questions to get the complete details. By just using a simple prop, such as your hand, you can always be ready to capture business.

Here is an example of what I have taught others when a call comes in. Memorize these questions using your fingers! I call it the "High Five."

Thumb—Thumbs up. "Hi! Great to get your call. Who referred you, and what made you decide to call me?"

First Finger—The number one thing you need to ask for is their contact information so you can stay CONNECTED! Ask for their email and phone number.

Middle Finger—You can think of it as the bird finger and ask the question: "Are you working with anyone currently? Do you have someone who has already been taking care of you?"

This gives you the chance to avoid wasting your time if they are already represented. Guide them back to their own rep, explain your ethics and values—and on to the next!

Ring Finger—The wedding finger represents the Mr/Mrs and the money. Ask whether they have their finances arranged, have they talked with their mortgage broker and also, is there a partner involved that you will be meeting?

Pinky Finger—Now you can ask about all the piddly little details, about what they need, what their timeline is, etc.

Write all of the details on your notepad and then put the sheet right into their new file. If you have an assistant, he or she can input the information into your Customer Relationship Management (CRM) Database. If the assistant is YOU, then add the information to your database as a lead!

"High Five" is an easy way to memorize the key questions, and you'll always be ready and professional when taking a call.

If you have ever lost a lead because of not being prepared or losing the random slip of paper on which you jotted down your notes, I know you will agree that having a streamlined process for connecting and keeping leads is imperative.

Don't lose another opportunity! Create this system for yourself now by trying out the "High Five" questions (or making up your own) and printing Lead Sheets to keep all your answers on. Keep a supply of these blank forms in a handy file folder in your office and in your vehicle.

Don't Be a Stranger

There's another little saying in sales: "When you meet someone for the first time, you're strangers; when you meet the second time, you're friends."

I know that some agents prefer a two-step market analysis for precisely this reason—they have an initial meeting and don't give their opinion on price until they see the clients for the second time, either at their home again or in the agent's office. Then, in meeting an old friend, they hope to acquire a new client.

If I were to suggest a new and improved strategy that will make your leads feel like friends when they meet you for the first time, would you be interested in hearing it?

Video.

The benefit of sending a quick message using today's technology will wow your leads and connect you to them right away. The benefits of video far surpass email or even a phone call! There are three, well-documented elements to communication: your words, your voice/tone, and your body language. We know that studies have shown that

- words only help communicate about 7 percent of what you mean;
- your voice and intonation help with another 38 percent; and
- it's your body language that drives home 55 percent of your message!

It only takes three minutes to create a little "Hello, I'm looking forward to meeting you tomorrow night! I will bring all the sales data from your neighbourhood and answer any questions that might be on your mind . . ." The potential clients will then have "met" you once, and when you arrive, they will feel as if they are meeting you for the second time.

You can verify this yourself by considering a news anchor or TV personality you watch. If you met them on the street, wouldn't you feel as if you already knew them? Certainly!

Use this strategy to your advantage, and you will be able to help more clients get the results they want by working with you!

You had me at Hello.
Connecting with Clients Immediately.

Do you remember Cupid?

This well-loved cherub, often the symbol of Valentine's Day, carries a bow and arrow and shoots an arrow into the heart of his victim, who is then believed to fall in love with the next person he or she sees.

What you might not know from Roman mythology is that Cupid isn't shooting love into people's hearts; he is actually creating a wound that makes them recognize that they are in pain. When they then see someone who meets their needs and heals their pain, they equate that person with the answer to their pain and fall in love.

If you want to know HOW to make your potential clients fall in love with you immediately, take a cue from history and start with their pain. I think the reason so many people fall for their doctor, nurse, or minister is precisely due to this concept. They are in pain and when someone helps them, they fall in love with their saviour.

But how will you know what pain your client is in if you go into your first sales presentation taking charge and telling them all about yourself and how great you are? I have seen many old-school agents take a binder to a presentation and go through it page by page—"Here I am, I am great, and I will sell your home! This is the company I work for, they are number one, and their brand will help sell your home . . ."

It doesn't matter how great you think you are, what matters is whether the clients feel that you can help them. Every client has unique needs and fears. Perhaps they have had many idiot agents in the past and are thinking of selling on their own. Perhaps they are worried that they won't be able to sell in time to move to another city and start a new job. It could be that the husband and wife aren't really on the same page and need some help in bridging the gap.

You won't know until you ask.

I always suggest to new agents that they start their first meeting with something like, "How can I help you?"—and then shut up! Let the clients share their hearts and thoughts so that you can meet their pain like a knight in shining armour!

Then they will fall in love with you.

CHAPTER 4

DAILY HABIT #2: A Big Business Needs a Big Foundation

In Calgary, Alberta, Canada, stands the Calgary Tower. It's a landmark and was quite the accomplishment in its day, standing 626 feet high in the heart of downtown. It weighs approximately 10,900 tons; however, 60 percent of that is underground. Over half of the structure is underneath the surface, supporting the height.

Often in business and life we only recognize the accomplishments we see above the surface. The tip of the iceberg, so to speak. We see skyscrapers looming high overhead, we see fruit ready to be picked off the tree, or we have, perhaps, a friend who is openly giving and friendly. But we cannot see what has gone on underneath or inside.

Preparations must be made if one wants to erect a high-rise. The fruit that gets picked every season is fed through a myriad of root structures that wind their way under the surface to nourish the growth. If a friend displays admirable qualities, there is no doubt that work has been accomplished on the inside first.

To build an impressive structure, product or reputation, you must have an appropriate foundation. For the Solopreneur, that foundation for business consists of the following.

1. Schedule lead-generation with good, custom scripts

For most successful salespeople, the foundation of their business lies in connecting with their leads and engaging them in conversation to see whether they can help by providing their services. Since your daily habits are what produce your yearly results, the number of people you talk to every single day adds up! As a professional, once you start a conversation, you also need to know exactly WHAT you want to say and have the ability to say it with confidence. Having a good "script" memorized (that you have tried out on family or friends) will help you feel prepared for anything potential clients may throw at you. This takes practice and effort, but if you want results, you need to put in the time!

Now don't assume I am referring to old-fashioned cold-calling scripts that people detest, such as "Are there any other decision makers?" or "Do you know anyone who wants to buy or sell in the next 60 days?" No! I am talking about you taking the time to pre-intend what you want to learn and share in your interaction. One of my favourite scripts is a mere "Hi, I was thinking about you today. How are you?" If you started out like this when calling your past clients, you would set the tone for relationship-building—rather than sounding like a needy sales call.

Think about what you like to hear from your service providers and make some scripts for yourself.

Schedule at least two or three calls a day, be confident and able to answer questions and concerns with intelligence.

2. Database follow-up

If you don't have a database to keep record of your clients and leads, then I will assume you must be in a government job! For the rest of us, we need help keeping in touch and keeping the details straight about each person we do business with. With all the amazing choices offered online, there is no excuse for not having a Customer Relationship Management (CRM) system. The one I have used in the real estate industry is called Top Producer, but there are many to choose from and to try out.

3. File-system management

You will need checklists and processes that are scalable and support every stage of your business. If you can take the details out of your head and put them on paper, you will come up with some brilliant checklists. You need to have a process that your business follows, right from the first interaction with a potential customer: following up, asking for the business, communication during your business together, and finally staying connected with each person in some unique and non-spammy way. Think of how you want your business to flow and implement your processes, systems, and checklists.

These core competencies may not seem all that glamorous, but without them, your business will implode under the weight of success.

Take your time, get the help you need, and build your foundation.

Everyday Mindful Millionaires

Alan Tennant, CEO Calgary Real Estate Board (CREB) 2016

Question: What does it take to be a successful Real Estate Agent?

I think one thing is that you really have to want it. And you have to clearly define what "it" is! You have to envision building the business and focus on the GOAL. On top of that, you need to find your community, or your tribe, and along the way, you must continually perfect your craft.

You have to pour everything you have into it, 24/7 for the first couple of years. And, as you gain traction, you learn to be more efficient, implement better systems, build a team, and implement growth.

The biggest mistakes I have witnessed were when entrepreneurs have had a lack of respect for their brand and reputation. There are no shortcuts that will give you long-term success. If you burn bridges and try to cut corners, you will never earn the kinds of referrals and recommendations it takes to succeed in real estate.

The best feeling in the business is when you reach a place where you can say "no" to a potential customer when there isn't a good fit. It is inevitable that you will come across personalities that just aren't a good fit with yours. If you can step back and recognize a mismatch and pass on the Listing or Purchase, you will be much better as an agent.

CHAPTER 5

DAILY HABIT #3: You Need to Scale or You Are Going to Fail

Just in case I have not yet convinced you to pay attention to your business base, let me remind you of what happened with Groupon. Groupon (and there are other lead-generating, coupon-style websites) offered small businesses an optimal opportunity to increase leads by offering the public discounted coupons for services. People were captured by the money-saving website and bought the product. The result was that all the businesses increased their customer base tenfold! Then do you remember what happened?

If any of you are like me, you might have had a similar experience. I bought a coupon for house cleaning. I called to redeem my coupon but couldn't get an appointment for over a month. Then when I finally received the service, it was terrible! It turned out that the cleaning company was so inundated with coupons they just didn't have the ability to service the large amount of volume! They weren't able to quickly scale up their business and very soon were out of business.

The hope for increased revenue resulted in just the opposite as customers received terrible service, and others couldn't arrange for service in a timely fashion. I heard over and over of many small businesses having to close up shop because the massive lead generation led to a system crash. If you think that all your business needs is more clients, think again.

Core competencies may not seem all that glamorous, but without them, your business will implode under the weight of success.

Have you ever had a job as a server, waitress, or bartender in the restaurant industry? There is a rhythm that you learn. When you start, you may feel as if you can only handle one table at a time. But soon enough, you learn how to juggle efficiently until you can handle a whole section of the restaurant!

Experienced salespeople have learned how to handle lots of business at the same time. They take new clients and feed them through their system: paperwork, product, sales, scheduled follow-up, negotiation of deals and finally, remaining connected to stay top of mind.

It takes time, effort, and practice to go from one deal a month to ten. Every time you feel overwhelmed, you must learn new skills that help you expand your capacity. However, it can take a few years to put systems into place that will help you juggle your business so that you can handle more.

Be diligent and implement one thing at a time. I would suggest that within three years you should be able to handle all the business you want—and that may include needing to hire your first administrative assistant!

They Left the Turkey Farm

How can you increase your confidence and possess what I like to call "sales esteem," when the voice in your heads keep reminding you that you are just a rookie?

At some point in your career, you will realize that you actually DO have something to offer; you will be able to feel confidence from your learned competency, and you will exude sales esteem.

Until then, you might have to fake it, till you make it.

SALES ESTEEM: "Acting Like a Pro even if You're a Novice."

I was watching a documentary on TV one day called Dirty Jobs, about working on a turkey farm. Now, I've always wondered about something I've heard concerning turkeys: If it's raining and a turkey looks up, it can drown!

Have you ever heard that?

The host interviewed a farmer about keeping turkeys, and it turns out that they die very easily and indeed, one of the ways can be from drowning when it rains! Who could believe that such a thing could happen? DEATH BY RAINDROP.

What a dismal existence for the turkey. Imagine if you had to walk around with your head down all the time, never looking up in case you might die!

I then asked myself what the best purpose for a turkey would be. Over Thanksgiving or Christmas, I'm sure a lot of us would agree on their best use—to fill our bellies! Also, the farmer said in the interview that since so many of them die all the time through natural causes, they end up making great fertilizer.

It seems then the best use for a turkey is either to be slaughtered and eaten, or die and be made into fertilizer so something else can grow—but not the turkey. So basically, they are more useful dead than alive!

Well, thank God we're not turkeys.

Speaking of turkeys, I'm reminded of the saying: "It's hard to soar with the eagles when you work with a bunch of turkeys."

If you want to soar with the eagles, don't be a turkey! Don't associate with those who mope around acting depressed, and don't make your home in the midst of death and worry.

The eagle is an interesting bird, however. Of course, a turkey can't even fly, but an eagle can soar higher than almost any other bird. Its vision is known to be six times greater than a human's. So, while it is soaring higher than other birds, it can see better than you or I! When it focuses on what it wants, it is concentrated, not distracted, and powers down to get what it's focused on.

Amazing.

I believe we were meant to soar with the eagles. But sometimes we end up feeling more like a useless turkey. Don't bring yourself down, and don't let others discourage you. Observe what the successful do and do as much of the same as you can. Follow the advice in this book and soon you will be soaring with your business and achieving the success you desire!

- Get off the farm.
- Be confident in your ability.
- Stay positive.
- Take action and execute your ideas!

Everyday Mindful Millionaires

Jeff Nunn, Manager of the hugely successful
Coldwell Banker in La Jolla, California

Question: What do you find are the biggest challenges for new agents?

The challenge I see for most is talking with potential sellers or buyers. Here they are, starting a new business, and they may not feel that they have enough knowledge or experience. What can they say to compete with the top producers? This is their ongoing challenge for about the first three years.

Two things we do to combat and conquer this challenge are role-playing and research.

In our office each week, agents practise with one another and try out various scripts and dialogues. They learn from other more experienced REALTORS® and gain their own experience along the way. Just like going to basketball practice, doing it over and over again WILL result in getting the ball in the hoop! Then, when they are in the game for real, the sales process will come more naturally, and hopefully new agents will feel more confident in their abilities, answers, and conversation.

Research is also a great way to instill confidence. If agents study the economy, know their numbers, and keep on top of the industry, they will fill themselves up with self-esteem, and this will help them feel comfortable when having those knowledge-based conversations with clients.

CHAPTER 6

DAILY HABIT #4: Learn About and Invest In the Best Tools

Let me encourage you to subscribe to the mindset that you need to buy things for your business. Yes, this is called an expense. I have met many Solopreneurs (and I have been one myself) who will do their best NOT to shell out an extra dime on anything. At some point, though, if you are going to build success, you will have to assign funds to help make your business grow.

Here Are Some Areas to Pay Attention to (and Possibly Pay Money to) so that Your Business Will Yield R.O.I.

Clarity

The key to being organized is the ability to be clear. What exactly needs to be done, how should it be done to save the most time and be the most efficient, and who is the best person to do it? You must start with being CLEAR on what you want for each task.

Do what you need to gain clarity. If it means hiring a coach, suck it up and do it. If you need to get away to the mountains and stay the weekend in business planning mode, do it. Take a successful business person out to lunch, talk to others you admire, attend conferences, etc.

A key to action is being clear.

Targeted SEO—whatever that means!

What a matrix of back-end analytics we have in the catch-phrase "SEO." I know some sales agents who pay big bucks for websites that draw in high activity via cold leads. They follow them up with immediate phone calls in hopes of capturing folks who find them online. For some, that business model works.

I know others who prefer a more authentic relationship with their online traffic and do this via consistent blogs, filled with local information and keywords used in searches.

Whatever model you choose, an active and responsive website, done correctly, is a necessity. So, don't be afraid of investing in what will be one of your most-seen marketing tools—your website.

Consistent Social Media

I am a fan of building social media profiles. Learn what you like yourself and then hire it out! Consistent, well-thought-out posts that show a variety of industry-related expertise, wise quotes, cute pics, and thought-provoking stats will build your contacts' trust in your brand. Just because you hire someone to implement this doesn't mean you are not in control of what goes out, and it certainly doesn't stop you from posting anything yourself. What it does is eliminate spur-of-the-moment, useless posts that don't help your image. Hiring it out also keeps you away from the social media black hole of time-wasting—where did the last hour go!?

Marketing

What are you doing annually to attract and retain business? Your answer should be outlined in an intentional marketing calendar. There is a saying in the advertising business that you have two choices: "Spray and pray," or "target and harvest." A big problem I often see for entrepreneurs concerns marketing. They have what they think is a good idea to bring in business; they will have postcards printed and mailed out and then wait for the business to roll in. The problem is that when you "spray and just pray," you are merely taking a chance that someone will be interested in calling you. What you need to do is decide on a plan. Build a campaign that uses multiple streams of touch points, such as snail mail, addressed mail, emails, phone calls, open houses, social media, etc. Make a concentrated effort to have each action build on the last.

For example, if you wanted to grow your real estate business in a certain neighbourhood, you could send out some branded mailers or flyers, and then follow up with mail to past clients in the area. Then hold an open house and drop off flyers to the neighbourhood homes, inviting folks to drop by. You could also send out an announcement on all social media and target some facebook ads to those postal codes. In this example, every step you take benefits from the last one and they build together.

Take enough time to strategically block a marketing calendar so you can have an assistant project-manage it for you. Or even hire a marketing expert to help you put some ideas in place that make sense (and literally make CENTS!).

Advertising

What exactly is advertising? Advertising is the last thing a Solopreneur should put his or her time and money into, in my opinion. Since so much business will be from the network that you know and from their recommendations, I usually put this on the back burner until all other avenues of the sales funnel are implemented. Once that happens and you want to allocate a bit of funds back into advertising, then do it with the same energy and purpose as your marketing. There are lots of local, community-based advertising opportunities such as newsletters, neighbourhood sports, fitness clubs, etc., that offer exposure where your audience is.

CRM/Database

Your database is what you need to keep track of every potential lead and certainly every single client. In it, you can keep notes on your history with them, schedule when to touch base, diarize important dates such as birthdays or sales anniversaries, and use it for mailing via snail mail or mass email. Your CRM can be free, cost a moderate monthly amount, or cost up to hundreds of dollars a month for the highest level program such as, Infusionsoft. Again, choose something and start using it!

E-Newsletters

This tool is used at regular intervals for keeping your presence in your network's top of mind. The benefit of using a tool like Mail Chimp or

Constant Contact is that these programs will allow you to see the analytics on the open rates and also give your sphere options to opt out. You can review who is actively looking at your emails, what headlines capture the most interest, and make the newsletters attractive with photos, videos, etc.

File Systems

I have found that most entrepreneurs don't love paperwork. But the smart ones do what needs to be done so they can be successful.

There is just no way around it, you must create a file system! I have helped many business owners create better filing systems by implementing only a few key processes. For one thing, if you use physical files for your clients while you work together, then choose a colour and keep it consistent.

In real estate, I advise most agents to have one coloured file for Sellers and another colour for Buyers. Having a visual differential is helpful when you are busy and need to find a client's file quickly.

If all your Sellers are green and your Buyers are blue, then you can also replicate this on your white boards in green and blue ink as you track the deals. Keeping your colours representative of your clients will greatly assist you in reading your key performance indicators.

You can also carry this colour-coding into your online calendar so everyone can see at a glance what type of activities are needing attention.

If you are paperless and keep all your clients online or in your computer, keep your files organized by having a main folder on your desktop, such as "Real Estate," and then inside sort your clients sensibly, such as putting "Buyers" and "Sellers" in separate folders. As the deals close, archive them in an annual folder (each year create, for example, an "Archived 2016" folder etc.) within the Sellers and Buyers folders.

Checklists

How do large organizations keep the wheels turning and business coming in? They have checklists for everything! Think of how precise McDonald's is when you order at the counter. In fact, one of their recent ads boasted that they were able to have teenagers running their restaurants. Want to know how they can trust their multi-billion-dollar corporate dollars in the hands of your children? Because everything is clear, and there is nothing left to guesswork.

Think about what you do for each client each time. Get the to-do lists out of your head and onto a checklist! Because each deal, each item, no matter how small, should be accounted for with a check mark when it is done.

The added benefit in creating your perfect checklists is that as you get busier, you can easily assign these tasks to your assistant. Once you have clarified exactly what needs to be done, and how each step is to be accomplished, you can have someone else take care of the details for you while you free up your time to go drum up more business!

White Boards/Smart Boards

For those of you who haven't worked with white boards, it is a great KPI (key performance indicator) that you can manage easily and set up at minimal cost. I have seen even large companies use a white board as an integral part of their systems. When I bought my first Mercedes, I sat in the financing office on the day of pick-up and filled out the paperwork. I looked around and noticed on the wall a large glass board divided into columns. Down the left side were all the surnames of purchasers, including mine. The next column had the date we were picking up our cars, and there were several columns for money amounts. There were check marks, notes, etc. I called attention to the board, and the finance associate said it was an important part of the process: Mercedes employees could look at the board and know at a glance where things stood with a client.

If it's good enough for Mercedes, I know it's good enough for your business too. Things like key approval dates, closing dates, expiry dates, tasks that are high priorities, and even whether you have received payment might be some topics you would find useful on a whiteboard.

I know one agent who painted her office wall with whiteboard paint so she could have a large enough space to track her clients!

Sales Package

I mentioned earlier about how old-school agents cart around a binder with page-by-page scripts of how great they are and how their brokerages are great too. Now let's talk about what you may find more valuable as part of your sales package.

No matter what your business, your future clients need to be able to see what it is you are going to do for them. To start with, let me ask you to do a short exercise. Ask yourself: what are the top three things clients need from me in my business?

____

(example: find me the right house.)

____

(example: price my house perfectly so it will sell soon.)

____

(example: negotiate the best price for me so I have the advantage.)

Think about special requests your leads might have. For example, if the client is a first-time home buyer, he may need basic real estate information; if he is from out of town, he may need information on the local process and rules. Clients want to feel that you are going to look after them, manage their expectations, and demonstrate to them why you think you can be of more service to them than the next guy.

Now that you have some ideas, what can you show prospective customers visually that exemplifies these things? Perhaps you could create a landing page on your website for new clients. And/or you could put together a folder with proof of your good work, samples of your product, etc. But everything that you display should exude excellence.

Don't cut corners when showing your value!

In my city, one of the most expensive neighbourhoods is dominated by a few local agents. At this moment, I can testify that none of these agents do anything special to create a nice feature sheet when they put a home up for sale. They just print the online listing details onto regular weight, 92 bright paper and leave 10 copies at the home for prospective buyers.

Any agent who wanted to take over that neighbourhood might use a pitch that included: "I know I might not be your number-one choice in this area to sell your home; you might feel that the long-time agents should be the ones you choose. But let me just share this: Avis, the car company, told people in their advertising that they were number two and added the slogan, "We Try Harder"! I can bet that my attention to marketing your home is better—just look at the effort put in to my feature sheets on this nice glossy paper with full-colour photos. Those long-time agents have been doing it for so long now that perhaps they don't care about selling as much as I do."

Something to think about when you are making a case for your services or product.

CHAPTER 7

DAILY HABIT #5: Always Remember to Swing Through

Be Long-sighted

In-the-know business owners recognize early on that success is part of a long-term plan. You can't count on making it rich quick! Your business plan should have 3-year, 5-year, and 10-year goals and end with a succession plan.

Being long-sighted in your business is nicely illustrated with an analogy to the game of golf.

I had the pleasure of speaking at a golf tournament a few years ago and while preparing for it, I asked if I could speak on the phone with the golf coach. He told me that one of the keys at the very core of how pros differ from amateurs in their game was their swing. Most novices pick their club and hit their ball with force so it will go as far as possible. But the professional has learned that his swing starts in the air behind him, and when he makes contact with the ball, he actually accelerates through the swing, not ending until he has made a full circle with the club.

After the lively chat with the golf coach, I couldn't help making the connection to business success with clients. Like a pro taking a swing, when you think of your clients, you must start long before they are working with you. And your goal at the end is that after the deal, you stay in touch and maintain a relationship until that client is referring new clients to you. Then you get to start the swing all over again. It is a perpetual swing that loops right back to where you started, over and over. It's like the song that never ends—but in a pleasant way.

Let me illustrate so it makes more sense.

One day a neighbour tells you that she has a friend who is looking for such and such (whatever your business is). She asks, "May I give her your number?"

You give her your card and respond with, "Here you are. Why don't I take her info so I can reach out when I'm at my desk."

You call Melissa, and indeed, she needs your help.

You begin working with her, addressing the issues she has; she falls in love with you; you complete a transaction.

Now, at this point, most salespeople wrap up the sale, say thank you, and cash their commission cheque! But when you are long-sighted, you know that you are not finished yet.

In fact, during the sales process there is an ideal time to discuss your services and ask for referrals from your current client. In real estate, this ideal time comes just after a sale is firm and everyone is happy. You are still in close contact, and this is the perfect time to let your client know how happy you are to have helped them and ask who else in their world might need you.

After the deal has closed, you have activities on your checklist that might include connecting with the client on social media, following up with a phone call to check in and asking whether they have any questions; you might add them to your monthly e-newsletter or insider email, perhaps send them something of value in the mail, or sign them up to a relevant magazine subscription, etc. After the deal is done, great agents continue building relationships and rapport UNTIL they are receiving referrals. It's about purposeful and consistent communication.

This mindset will create a business you can build a career on!

I know a good handful of Solopreneurs who have taken such great care at the end of their sales cycle to swing through, so that now, at the age of retirement, they are finding themselves at the height of their careers because the momentum is so strong—it has been driving the business with referrals over and over again. They could easily retire, but their clients still want and need them. Imagine being able to do something you love past retirement that continues to bring in good money. They have set themselves up for success, and you can do the same!

Accelerate through the swing while in the deal process and then at the end, Swing THROUGH!

The measure of who we are is what we do with what we have.

Vince Lombardi

SECTION III

MASTERY OF SOLO SUCCESS

A Sales Professional who Figured it Out!

David left a corporate career to go Solopreneur about four years ago. Were his wife and two daughters worried about the risky change of direction? I don't know, but what I do know is this man had a plan to succeed and he did it!

The benefit that David's previous career in Corporate Accounts had given him was an insight into marketing and consistency. He didn't know everything about running a real estate business, but what he did know he did to the highest degree of excellence—and what he didn't know, he learned along the way. In the first year, he hired my services to review and help implement systems and processes so that he would be able to handle a heavy workload without being buried underneath it.

He spent targeted time perfecting his checklists, we created systems for diarizing important closing dates, and he learned how to properly manage a new database. He spent time and money on an amazing website that projected a professional image. He learned sales scripts that he could use with confidence. And, he churned the business.

In looking back, I believe part of David's success was due to his mindset. He understood and accepted the fact that success would take several years and building up a clientele would be an investment which would take time to grow.

At the end of the third year, he called me to report that he was so busy (at over 60 deals that year) that he realized it was time for him to hire his first assistant. With the same astute concentration, we prepared his business to add help, and over several months I assisted him in interviewing and assessing candidates until a good fit was found and added to his team.

There were certainly roadblocks initially that he didn't know how to overcome. But his courage and tenacity helped him to find the answers he needed. Today he is one of the top agents in his brokerage with a stellar reputation. It didn't happen by accident; it happened on purpose and with purpose!

You can do this too—take what you know and the time to learn what you don't from the experts! You must also realize that it can take three to five years to build a new business. So, have the patience and tenacity to think long-term success rather than short-term riches.

Have the patience and tenacity to think long-term success rather than short-term riches.

CHAPTER 8

Overcome What is Holding You Back

"But I can't! This is standing in my way." Even with ALL the information at your fingertips, there may still be a small voice in your head whispering your worries. I know that when I started my consulting business, my history with bankruptcy really limited my belief that I could earn a living doing what I love! Stepping away from being an employee to being the owner of my own business felt like a big risk. And for a few years, I had to chase away the naysayers in my head.

I adopted a brilliant meditative breathing exercise that could bring me into the present moment and help me to see my path more clearly—rather than getting my knickers in a knot and freaking out. I'd like to share it with you.

In his book, *Your Survival Instinct is Killing You*, Marc Schoen, PhD, details a technique he developed for patients who were in an acute state of stress. Using this exercise, he says, enables you to reduce your stress significantly, in as little as a minute.

Try his exercise when you feel your doubts trying to overtake your dreams.

> Get comfy and plant your feet on the ground. He says it doesn't matter whether your eyes are open or closed, whichever is more comfortable.
>
> Inhale slowly for 3 to 5 seconds. While you breathe in, focus your attention on feeling light and airy.
>
> Don't let all of your breath out at once; force it out bit by bit. Imagine a balloon full of air. If you hold the end and open it just a little, the air will force its way out in a noisy, condensed fashion. Purse your lips and open them just a bit; now push out 3 seconds of air. It will make a sound as you push it through the tiny hole between your lips.
>
> Then stop for 2 or 3 more seconds.
>
> Then push it out again for 3 seconds.
>
> Continue in this way until you have released all of the breath.
>
> Inhale and exhale for a few breaths in a relaxed fashion.
>
> Repeat the exercise, stopping and starting the release of air.

If you repeat the exercise four to six times in a row, Dr Schoen says your stress level will decrease, you will feel a lower level of agitation, and your heart will beat more slowly.

It's a simple technique that I find works quite well whether I am driving, closing a sale, preparing to speak, or being agitated by family! I'm sure that everyone could benefit from having a technique like this in their back pocket. Keep calm and breathe on!

When all seems to be going wrong, stop and remain still.

If you get to a point of doubt and despair, change direction immediately and put down your weapons! It's normal to come up against giant problems or fears that feel overwhelming and discouraging. At these times (desperate times call for desperate measures) drop what you're doing and take a moment—or a day, or even a week.

If you feel as if you're hitting your head against a brick wall, perhaps you are! I would strongly encourage a day away to meditate, be silent with yourself, and let go of everything—be in the moment and hit the reset button. Drive out to the mountains and have a picnic, go to the beach and just be alone, find a cool stream and spend a day breathing and releasing.

No one can chart your destiny except you. But sometimes we get ourselves into a funk and end up sabotaging the good that's going on. When this happens, don't try to force success; do the opposite. Let go, drop the ball, get into nature and find your grounding again.

Whatever you want to do in this world must first be done within.

Then, when you are again in your present mind, go ahead and face your fears—and solve them.

Here are some problem areas that entrepreneurs regularly struggle with, and some suggestions for solving them. Perhaps you can relate.

Time—Do you need more time?

Many of us feel we need more of it! For example, you may be working as an employee and trying to start your own business on the side.

Consider this.

It's a fact that if you got out of bed 30 minutes earlier during the workweek, you would create for yourself 10 extra hours of valuable time each and every month!

If you stopped wasting time on too much social media, video games, daydreaming and procrastinating, you could create at least two more targeted hours per day to get practical things done! If you did that during the workweek, you would add another 20 whole days per year!

If, instead of winding down after dinner by tuning in to the TV until bedtime, you took just one hour (after quality time visiting with your loved ones) and used it for some targeted business efforts, that one extra hour, 5 nights per week, would create 240 extra hours annually (20 extra hours every month)!

So, create more time for yourself if that is what you need.

Connections—Is this a stumbling block you need to make into a stepping stone to get your results?

If you need connections, who would they be, where are they, and who do you already know that could connect you if you just asked?

I remember when I wanted to start speaking at real estate conferences. I applied for three years in a row to present a session at a national conference. Every year my application was denied. I became frustrated and feared that I would never be able to break in! Then I considered trying something different.

I asked myself what OTHER conferences needed speakers and with a quick Google search found some major events closer to where I lived, and I spoke there. Then I asked myself what brokers I knew who might have industry connections to the organizers of the national conference. I kept uncovering possibilities. (There really is truth to the idea of six degrees of separation!) Over a couple of months, I met and had coffee with two leaders who not only had heard me present at local conferences but also were connected to organizers of a Western conference! I asked for a referral, I followed up, I connected with the organizer on social media, I phoned and followed up with an email.

I was hired to speak for TWO sessions at the conference!

I had been banging on the door with one idea in my head with no results. So, eventually I realized I needed to open my mind to new ideas and tap into the connections I currently had to reach out to the ones I wanted.

It can work for you too. Do it!

Money—Do you need more money?

I challenge you to search within yourself and you WILL come up with the right ideas.

I remember Christmastime one year. I had finally gotten an office job, but it was taking so long to get back on my feet again—and then I looked at my calendar and realized with dismay that Christmas was coming up! I have never been one for giving extravagant gifts, but with four teens, even an extra $400 for gifts would break my bank. I searched and considered many options and finally decided that I would apply for a second job at Chapters since I liked books. That year, guess what everyone received for presents? Half-price books with my employee discount! Nevertheless, I had put my idea into action and gotten just enough extra income to give gifts and enjoy a turkey dinner.

Yes, retail jobs suck—you know it! But if your goal is clear in your mind, you will come up with ideas that are right for you, and you will do what must be done! As the saying goes,"You can't steer a parked car."

I believe that our actions and our ability to choose to move forward create a whole host of activities which we don't understand and may not even know anything about—but forward momentum causes a ripple effect that is undeniable. Action trumps fear.

Believe it. Do it.

With that comes an ability, or decision really, to make yourself do what others choose not to.

"If it were easy, everyone would do it!" Nothing can stand in your way, except yourself.

Turn your stumbling blocks into
stepping stones.

CHAPTER 9

Celebrate Your Victories!

A great way of motivating is giving yourself rewards for reaching your goals. Give yourself a pat on the back every so often. Since you are usually the only one keeping yourself accountable, you may also be the only one who knows when you have something to celebrate!

The first year I worked with the Tanya Eklund Group, Tanya herself joined an elite group of entrepreneurs on a visit to Richard Branson's Nekker Island. She witnessed first-hand how this extraordinarily successful icon took purposeful recreation time and celebrated successes! She spent time on his paradise island with other high achievers and focused entrepreneurs. Their time included working ON their businesses as well as celebrating their accomplishments. Tennis, boating, water sports and custom cocktails with a delectable menu was the experience of a lifetime! That year, Tanya had the best year of her career. Was it due solely to that trip? Certainly not. The real estate market was good that year, she had great support, and she followed excellent business practices. But we can't discount the effect of being inspired and motivated by some of the best examples in the world. Just the fact that she valued herself enough to participate in the excursion makes a statement about her frame of mind.

It's okay to work hard, but it's also necessary to allow yourself to play hard.

How can we argue with the results achieved by those top entrepreneurs who really know how to play hard and celebrate successes?

I'm sure you can think of many great ideas that would help you celebrate your business victories. Perhaps it's a coveted brand of clothing, a trip to Vegas, dinner at an amazing restaurant, a day trip to a beautiful spot, or a personal service such as teeth whitening or a deep facial. Pick something that motivates you and start keeping track! After all, don't they say that life is about the journey and not just the destination?

I was listening to Eckhart Tolle in my car last week while driving to an appointment and was reminded that if we are only focused on the end result—making two million, closing 100 deals, finishing our degree, taking our next vacation, and so on—we are not taking advantage of being in the present moment. Eckhart reminds us that the whole power of being and succeeding is learning how to be content in our present moment.

So, listen up, take those moments and celebrate along the way! In doing this, you are helping your business and yourself become better!

A well-known quote of Richard Branson says:
You can only live once. And I just don't want to waste a minute of my life.

CHAPTER 10

Communicating at the Highest Level

I received a call from an agent looking for a strategy. He had been interviewed by potential clients about six months prior but was not chosen to list their home. He was very disappointed. They listed with someone else, but their home did not sell. When he phoned to tell me that these clients were giving him another chance, we got to work!

We went over what had happened at his first appointment. Brad arrived prepared, he viewed the home, he went through his presentation page by page, and then asked whether they had any questions. He felt that he'd done a good job.

I suggested that he change just one thing this time: before starting his presentation, he should start with looking them in the eyes and ask, "Tell me what is important to YOU."

He called me the next day, thrilled with how his meeting had gone and indeed, he subsequently got the chance to list the home!

Now, what had made the outcome different? Brad was still the same person. He still had the same information in his presentation. The only thing that changed was his approach to the homeowners in putting their needs first.

Let me illustrate by drawing an analogy to the sound system at a concert. Have you ever enjoyed an evening listening to your favourite band on stage? I used to sing in a band, and I can tell you this: what the audience hears is very different from what the musicians hear.

There are monitors on the stage that face the musicians. Each band member can ask the sound person to increase the volume through his or her monitor to accentuate what is important for that musician to hear and to decrease the volume of the other musicians. As a singer, it was important to me to hear myself and the notes I was hitting as well as the bass guitar and the other singer. The rest of the music was in the background. That arrangement enabled me to give my best performance.

On the other hand, the audience hears a professionally put-together mix of all the instruments and singers. If they were to hear only one monitor, it would be quite a disappointing event!

So, when you are the rock star going to your sales appointment, I know there are things that you feel are important for you to say. But unfortunately, if it's the sound of your own voice being heard the whole time, you may lose the client! All the information that is in your own mind, that you have researched, and what you consider important, may not be as important to your audience. If you can tune in to what your audience wants to hear, then you can adjust the mix and add in the notes that are relevant to them, rather than giving them the whole concert through your monitor.

So, be aware that what YOU think is important and relevant may not be to your client. You don't know their history or their concerns, and you might not have the scoop on why they need to sell or buy. Without all of the details, how can you possibly tailor a presentation just for them?

For the professional who earnestly wants to take his or her service up a notch: practise tuning in to the needs of your clients and give them time to share their true wishes with you. If you take care to do this right, like Brad, you will find that the leads who had no interest in working with you before will suddenly be knocking at your door.

CHAPTER 11

Beware the Momentum Killers

The only time you coast is when
you are going downhill.

Tim Gard

It's one thing to get to the top; it's another to keep your business there! I have worked side by side with some extreme producers and this is what I have seen nipping at their heels to distract or drive their business off the rails. Beware of these three momentum killers.

1. Resting on Your Laurels

The dictionary defines this phrase as:

> *To rely on one's past achievements instead of working to maintain or advance one's status or reputation.*
>
> *To be so satisfied with your achievements that you make no effort to improve.*
>
> Copyright© Cambridge University Press 2003

Note: Laurel is a plant—the aromatic Laurus Nobilis tree. In ancient times, the leaves were formed into a ring and worn on top of the head as a symbol of victory.

When you reach a goal, what do you do? If you won a victory, for example, you grossed two million dollars, is it not a natural thing to react by putting your feet up on the desk, leaning back and thinking, that was a good year; now I can relax, and it will happen again next year.

Perhaps it isn't as conscious as that, but if you adopt that attitude, it will bite you in the ass. If you want to keep up momentum and reproduce excellent results, be sure to never relax by resting on your laurels.

A friend, who had her house up for sale, called me. She had hired a well-known husband and wife real estate team who had been around for years and had a good reputation. But as the days and weeks went by, she was questioning her decision.

Her experience dealing with the team was quite a bit different from what she had expected. For example, when she received feedback after home showings, the team merely forwarded her the direct, unedited texts from the other agents. My friend found this feedback to be a little too brash. I had to wonder myself why they wouldn't have revised or rewritten the comments before sending them to their client. I presumed they had become so familiar with the industry, perhaps a little tired in making the extra effort, that they didn't take the time to ask themselves what would be best for their client.

During the negotiations when the first offer came in, the agent expressed to my friend how overwhelmed and busy they were, how they had three deals on the go and had lost two already, and how he was feeling really stressed! My friend, who is also a professional salesperson, suggested that he make her deal go through rather than striking out three times!

When she came to me, she was distressed and thought their management of her sale seemed very lazy and they were treating her with much too familiarity.

I had to agree.

Clients want and need to be treated as special, and they deserve to have details explained properly. Whenever there are tough negotiations underway, agents need to provide a filter, rather than bringing their clients to the inner circle.

Be careful about resting on your laurels; there will always be someone in the wings waiting to swoop in and treat your clients better. Remember that song by Toby Keith? "Hold my beer, while I kiss your girlfriend . . ."

2. Cotton-Eyed Joe

On the subject of country songs, there is a song that asks:

If it hadn't been for Cotton-Eyed Joe,
I'd been married a long time ago.
Where did he come from? Where did he go?
Where did he come from, Cotton-Eyed Joe?

How do you keep your priorities from getting trumped by shiny objects like this Cotton-Eyed Joe? Where did this distraction come from? In the song, someone was going to be married, but Cotton-Eyed Joe got in the way!

I have seen good business owners drawn too close to the light, and like a moth to the flame, learn a painful lesson about becoming distracted.

An increase in net worth allows more opportunities, such as investments, philanthropy, and even new business pursuits. But just as it took all your attention to get to where you are in your business, it will also take a great deal of focus to bring other projects to success. If you think that you have a finely tuned machine that can drive the business while you pursue other avenues, think again.

To let go of your current business long enough to make money at something else requires a whole new set of competencies. I'm not saying it can't be done, but for most Solopreneurs, it is a shift to something new.

I would caution against the "squirrel" temptation—scattering your wealth in too many places. Of course, once you have reached a certain level of wealth, you will want to expand to other investments. But do so consciously, once you have excellent systems in place that will not let anything fall through the cracks while your attention is divided among other streams of income.

Some Solopreneurs find new investments close to their own industry, such as providing financing for second mortgages. Some become investors, providing seed capital for something they believe in. Others might consider starting a new business online or on the side. Still others might become a coach or speaker due to their success. These are all noble pursuits.

If and when these opportunities arise, remember that when you take your attention away from your primary business, it will have an impact. If you want to keep the momentum steady, then many safeguards will have to be put into place. This may include using technology better, hiring the best of the best to run your business, partnering with others, and so on.

So, before you jump in with both feet, perhaps not realizing the full impact on your current business, take a step back and evaluate. Then take actions that will keep you focused on what is most important and what will yield the best results.

However, to keep on the safe side, I would advise you to stay away from shiny objects trying to lure you into the burning flame!

3. Suffering By Not Building a Good Team

I spoke once at a conference called NexGen Rebar Camp. It was a kind of reverse conference in that it held many sessions in smaller rooms so that the emphasis could be on collaboration, questions, and sharing. I hosted a session on Turning Support Staff into Support Stars. One thing the organizer confessed to everyone was that she wished she had built a team sooner in her career.

As Solopreneurs, we sometimes put ourselves in solitary confinement! We work from our home office, we email correspondence, we get contracts signed electronically. We go for days without being in contact with another human being! Do you realize that in prison this kind of exclusion is the worst punishment?

Building your team is a step towards a legacy of success. As soon as you have clarified your tasks within systems, delegating can mean finding freedom. But it doesn't end there. Once you have hired staff, you become the manager, the leader of your team, and if you don't have experience, how will you know what to do?

One of the best things a business owner can do is LEARN how to become a better leader!

The best leaders make painstaking efforts to get the right staff in place and aren't afraid to "hire slow and fire quick." They are clear in their expectations and keep the reins in their hands until they have tested the trustworthiness of their employees. The best leaders have developed an amazing ability to bring out the best in their team by encouraging them to grow as individuals and to take ownership of the tasks they excel at. I know one team whose boss sent them all to a Robin Sharma conference—now that's putting your money where your mouth is!

If you follow through on these steps with your team, you will find yourself at the top of the roster—and don't be surprised if you start receiving calls from more extraordinary people wanting a job on your team.

Note the Steps:

- Set Clear Expectations.
- Train thoroughly.
- Give Scheduled Reviews.
- Appreciate Staff Regularly.

Everyday Mindful Millionaires

Grady Topak, YYC Cycle (*Spin Cycle Studio*)

Advice for Entrepreneurs!

- Be clear on your clients' expectations: "expectations are the root of all heartaches."
- Give concierge style of service.
- Make clients feel when they work with you that they've become part of your tribe, your family, your gang (YYC Cycle has a Biker "gang").

Momentum Booster!

When I started my career in the real estate industry, I read Barbara Corcoran's book, *If You Don't Have Big Breasts, Put Ribbons on Your Pigtails: And Other Lessons I Learned from My Mom*. That was before Barbara became a celebrity Shark on NBC's *Shark Tank*. In her book, she brilliantly tells the story of how she became a millionaire real estate agent. My recollection of it centres around her being fed up with being a waitress, of working for other people, and with not being in control of her own success. She borrowed money from her then-boyfriend and started a real estate business. When they parted ways, he told her she would never make it without him. That made her so angry she set out to prove him wrong about her ability to succeed. That motivation spurred her on to sell a building of undesirable units which gave her the traction she needed to move forward to a successful business.

Think about your own motivation for succeeding. Does it carry enough weight to catapult you forward as Barbara's did her?

If you can dig deep, reach your goals, and create a sustainable career, you could also step forward and become a celebrity. For example, when you are in your best years and grossing over two million dollars in commissions, you could accelerate into the limelight, should you wish to do so.

If you find that you are being contacted regularly by new agents asking whether you have a spot on your team for them, or perhaps whether they can take you for coffee to pick your brain, you may have reached a level that others esteem. You could use that trajectory to take you to the "Celebrity Level."

In my opinion, it would be wise to first focus your influence on the general public (potential clients) by engaging in social media messages, creating a following, hosting video programs, and starting a YouTube channel. You could even begin offering regular seminars at a local meeting place. Get out there, get your name seen, and share your good reputation with the public.

When you start getting calls at your office from people who answer the question, "How did you find me?" by saying, "Oh, I see you everywhere!", you know you are on the right track.

Once you are feeding your sales funnel with regular clients and have implemented reliable systems and also built a trustworthy team, you might also consider sharing yourself within your industry. Barbara Corcoran reaches out to real estate agents by offering her advertising services. So does Frederick Eklund with the TV show, *Million Dollar Listing*, New York, and his best-selling book, *The Sell.* You could start by sharing your business model in a class at your local Real Estate Board. Perhaps you will be inspired to write a book sharing your story to impact others. Or you might speak at annual industry conferences. There are a number of ways to take your current success and launch it even further by becoming a celebrity.

If becoming a celebrity is something you are considering, here is an easy three-step plan.

> **First** — *Speak to your Brokerage and Board about preparing a session on whatever part of your business is the most interesting to you. Tap into your own passion and write up a little 45-minute seminar that you would be willing to share with others wanting to get to your level.*
>
> *When you speak at your sessions, have a sign-up sheet to collect email addresses and add them to an industry Customer Relationship Management Database that you can start using regularly.*
>
> **Second** — *Write your book! Spend a year jotting down things you think would be interesting to other sales agents in your industry. Then come up with a 20,000-word manuscript (it will happen in no time!). Hire a professional editor and either self-publish or locate a publisher or publishing service for more professional help. Becoming an author adds huge credibility to your reputation and will impress your clients as well as your peers!*

Third — *Take your book and seminar and offer to speak at conferences all over the world! Sharing your passion and your message is what the world needs, and you are the only one who can tell your story! And who knows, one day your phone may ring with an offer to participate in a new TV show about entrepreneurs. Becoming a celebrity agent is for those who want to deal with the top in their city!*

CHAPTER 12

You've Always Had the Power

In Chapter 2 we talked about *The Wizard of Oz* and the need for brains, heart, and courage. I now want to remind you of the end to that story.

Dorothy and her friends finally arrive in the Emerald City. They've overcome all the roadblocks. They make it! A big sigh of relief from the group, I'm sure.

But in a profound revelation, they discover that the "Mighty Wizard" is a fake! There is no omnipotent Oz who can make their dreams come true.

Then comes the big aha moment when the Good Witch explains to Dorothy, "You had the power all along."

Friends, I have never heard more meaningful words. YOU are the wizard of your life! YOU are the one who connects with the dream inside your heart, YOU create a vision in your head of where you want to go, and it is YOU who must take action to get yourself there, if it is important enough for you.

Is there a God (or Wizard) involved? I will leave the spiritual answers up to each of you; for me, life has been and continues to be an incredible, spiritual journey. For years I had hoped, prayed and WISHED that my God, or someone, would find me and take me where I wanted to go, give me a good job, put me on TV, hire me to write a book. I prayed fervently that a miracle would happen to bring about my destiny. I didn't think I had the capacity to achieve these desires on my own.

After watching *The Wizard of Oz*, I realized that it was I who wore the magic ruby slippers and had the power all along! That realization gave me a huge boost in taking responsibility for making my own dreams come true. I wouldn't wait any longer for someone else to open the doors to the Emerald City or get me home to Kansas. I would open the doors myself and walk through! And now that I know I have it, I want to share the magic with others.

You don't need to stay where you are; you can pursue your own destiny.

There are two kinds of pain we experience in life. There is either the pain of discipline, or the pain of regret.

Jim Rohn

CHAPTER 13

Blooper Reel

I often enjoy ending a good movie by watching the bonus blooper reel. For your post-reading pleasure, I here present some true, embarrassing moments from real agents in the industry!

A man I worked for was getting older and his hair was starting to grey. Being Italian with a thick black mane, he wondered whether he should do something about it—and, if so, what? An acquaintance mentioned that she had her hair coloured at a salon and suggested that he go; it was so easy! So, sheepishly, he made an appointment with her hair stylist and asked to have the grey covered. The dye and hair foils were applied. As he sat there in all his glory, one of his esteemed female rivals walked in to the same salon to have her hair done—and saw him.

He was never so embarrassed in his life! He never got his hair coloured again for fear of a repeat experience.

I worked with a beautiful celebrity agent for a couple of years who dressed to the nines each and every day. Her hair was always beautifully coiffed, she wore designer dresses, and she loved a good, high-heeled shoe.

One day she was at her desk waiting for a client to arrive. She heard someone walking up the hall so she got up to meet him. As she walked toward the door, she caught her heel on the plush area rug and did a face-plant as the client came through her door! She was mortified, but jumped up like a gymnast and brushed it off as if nothing had happened.

The area rug was removed the next day!

A top-producing husband and wife team who served millionaire clients sold a lovely acreage home. When they met with the family to take possession, everyone was shocked to discover, in the backyard, chickens in a chicken coop! How about that? A new home and fresh dinner included!

I had the pleasure of consulting for a customer-focused team of two men, one who had been in the business for more than twenty years. He had recently brought in a junior partner to train up to take over the business. They were diligent in adhering to the processes they had in place, and one thing they always were careful about was getting condo documents prior to receiving an offer on a property.

A client had been asked to submit his condo docs several times, but was tardy in gathering them together. Finally, the junior partner went to the client's apartment to pick them up and was handed a huge file folder with a mess of paperwork. When he brought it back to the office, he gave it to his assistant to organize.

The administrative assistant was shocked to discover several porn DVDs in the file. She asked the agent what that was all about! Boy, did they all have a good laugh!

While having a conversation with an agent in Washington, I was told this story she had heard from one of her associates.

A guy in my office was showing a home we had toured earlier that day together as part of a REALTOR® Caravan. He was especially impressed with the master suite and could not get hold of his clients fast enough to see this fabulous home.

He left a message with the seller, as indicated in the MLS, that he would be showing the house and took his clients to see it. He was beaming as he showed the great features of the custom home. As they walked down the hallway to the master, he said, "You are not going to believe your eyes!"

He swung the door wide open, and to their surprise, two teenagers, who were obviously skipping school, were sharing a little "afternoon delight." At first mortified, and then scared, the naked teens began to scream bloody murder, thinking it was some kind of home invasion.

The clients were screaming too, and the Realtor began to laugh hysterically. BUSTED. He now has a habit of KNOCKING on every door he encounters—even in vacant homes.

Everyone has bloopers in their life—those times that are embarrassing at the moment, but you can laugh about later on. I would encourage you to keep a record of those moments for yourself; it's fun and entertaining to look back—and who knows, one day you might want to write a book!

HIGHLY RECOMMENDED READING

There is a world of discovery right at our fingertips for those who will pick up a book and turn the pages. Through others' tales of experience, frustration, challenges, and victory, we too find the answers and inspiration we need to go forward and succeed in life and business.

Here is my personal favourite reading list of books that have made the biggest impact in my life!

- The Bible
- The Power of Focus, Les Hewit
- If You Don't Have Big Breasts, Put Ribbons on Your Pigtails, Barbara Corcoran
- Integrity, Dr Henry Cloud
- Growing Your Business, Mark LeBlanc
- Millionaire Real Estate Agent, Gary Keller
- The Greatest Salesman in the World, Og Mandino

ABOUT THE AUTHOR

Sue Styles is an author, speaker, and Real Estate Business Coach.

Since 2004, she has worked hands on behind the scenes in the offices of many top teams and individuals, coaching them to better results. This includes the #1 Team at the #1 RE/MAX Brokerage in the world, in Calgary, Alberta.

Sue is an instructor with her local Real Estate Board and has helped develop a successful unlicensed administrative course. She teaches new agents to build their businesses and seasoned veterans to stay at the top!

Her book for administrative assistants, *Be Extraordinary—Right Where You Are*, has been sold at the National Association of REALTORS® annual conferences.

Sue continues to help Solopreneurs be successful in their businesses. Perhaps yours will be next!